WELLINGTON

FROM ABOVE

To the memory of a great Wellingtonian and friend
Peter Neville La Vie Findlay 1940 – 2009

Previous page: Somes/Matiu Island, silhouetted against the
morning sun on Wellington Harbour, as the *Torea* departs the port.

First published 2011

GRANTHAM HOUSE PUBLISHING
6/9 Wilkinson Street
Wellington 6011
NEW ZEALAND

Copyright © Graham Stewart

ISBN   978 1 86934 115 2

A catalogue record for this book is available
from the National Library of New Zealand.

The right of Graham Stewart to be identified as the author of this work in terms
of section 96 of the Copyright Act 1994 is hereby asserted.

Edited by Lorraine Olphert

Design and concept by Graham Stewart,
Bookprint Consultants Limited, Wellington
Printed by Bookprint International Limited

WELLINGTON
FROM ABOVE

Graham Stewart

GRANTHAM HOUSE

New Zealand

Contents

Facing page and above: WELLINGTON RAILWAY STATION –
The busiest station in the country; 37,000 commuters pass
through the complex daily.

LOOKING DOWN ON THE HEART of the central business district.

The Police launch *Lady Elizabeth III was commissioned in 2010.*

PARLIAMENT BUILDINGS – The Beehive (1982) and the northern wing with the dignified central colonnade (1922), the entrance to Parliament Buildings. The building is faced with South Island Takaka marble. Beyond is the classic neo-Gothic building which houses the General Assembly Library.

THE HIGH COURT AND THE CATHEDRAL OF ST PAUL – Molesworth Street. The Wellington Anglican Cathedral of St Paul was originally designed in the 1930s by Christchurch architect Cecil Wood; the foundation stone was laid by Queen Elizabeth II in January 1954. The first stage of construction was dedicated in May 1964. The final design was by the renowned New Zealand architect Sir Miles Warren. The Cathedral was completed in 1998. The High Court (foreground), was opened in September 1993.

THE SUPREME COURT – The new building, opened in January 2010, on the corner of Whitmore Street and Lambton Quay, is linked with the restored former High Court building. Built in 1879, it was the first major public building in Wellington to be constructed in masonry (brick and concrete) rather than wood since the earthquake of 1855. The decorative bronze screen that surrounds the new building is inspired by the intertwining of pohutukawa and rata. The exterior screen is eight metres high and has 88 panels, each one made of 17 pieces.

BOWEN HOUSE – The second generation Bowen House (1990) on the corner of Lambton Quay and Bowen Street is 22 storeys high. It was the temporary home of Parliament's debating chamber while the 1922 Parliament Buildings were being refurbished in the 1990s.

STATE HIGHWAY ONE (SH1) cuts through the suburb of Thorndon as it enters the city.

THE INNER CITY BYPASS at the southern end of the city cuts through Te Aro. Southbound traffic feeds into Vivian Street, while motorists travelling north out of the city enter from Karo Drive.

WESTPAC STADIUM – the heart of capital sport and entertainment. A Rugby World Cup 2011 venue, the stadium is host to five pool matches and two quarter-finals. The 35,000-seat cantilever-roofed stadium stands where Aotea Quay meets Waterloo Quay, only a short walk from the city centre. Wellington boasts the largest number of bars and restaurants per capita in New Zealand and is known for the public parties it stages for sporting events and live entertainment.

LOOKING SOUTH OVER THE CENTRAL BUSINESS DISTRICT to the international airport on the horizon with the Wellington urban motorway (SH1) in the foreground.

INTERISLAND FERRY TERMINALS. Two companies, the government-owned Interislander Line and Strait Shipping Limited, which operates the Bluebridge ferry service (above), compete for passenger, freight and car business across Cook Strait between Wellington and Picton with roll-on/roll-off ferries. Below is the Interislander *Kaitaki* which entered service in 2005.

QUEENS WHARF was once the gateway to the city when people and produce arrived by sea. Today the wharf and surrounding area have been developed into a public playground of parklands and restaurants. Beyond the sails is the TSB Bank Arena, used for cultural and indoor sporting events, is the venue for the annual Montana World of Wearable Art Awards. By the entrance to the TSB Bank Arena is the Olympic Museum Gallery.

HISTORIC WHARF SHEDS 13 AND 11 on Customhouse Quay, built in 1904 of brick with plaster facings on the wharf precinct.

Facing page: THE COPPER REFLECTIONS of city buildings on the Intercontinental Wellington on Customhouse Quay. In the distance down Waterloo Quay is the Westpac Stadium and the cruise ship *Crystal Serenity* berthed at Aotea Quay. Customhouse Quay is now lined with pohutukawa trees right down the centre which add colour during the summer months.

Facing page: ROOF-TOP BARBECUE AREAS on the roof of the Wharf Offices Apartments are a feature of inner-city living in the 21st century.

FEATHERSTON STREET in the centre of the central business district. Now dwarfed by surrounding buildings, the Dominion Farmers' Institute building

FEATHERSTON STREET reflected in the glass towers of modern Wellington.

LAMBTON QUAY follows the curve of the original shoreline - loose metal then tarseal replaced the sand on the foreshore in the 19th and 20th centuries. The first wooden structures were followed by splendid wooden and masonry buildings before the giant buildings that reach skywards today.

THE FORMER PUBLIC TRUST BUILDING on the corner of Lambton Quay and Stout Street is a superb Edwardian baroque building, designed by the Government architect J. T. Campbell and built in 1908. The building was sold by the Public Trust in 1981.

PEDESTRIANS AND REFLECTIONS IN THE HEART OF LAMBTON QUAY – a glass tower building opposite Kirkcaldie and Stains department store reflects the midday sun and the busy street below.

Facing page: Suburban buses drop shoppers on the golden mile of retail shopping.

OPEN-AIR ROOFTOP PRIVATE RETREATS are a feature of many inner-city buildings.

Facing page: THE STATE INSURANCE TOWER, built to house the head office of the Bank of New Zealand, was given the nicknames 'Darth Vader's pencil box' or 'the great safe deposit box in the sky' when opened. Designed in the late 1960s, it was not occupied until 1984 due to industrial disputes. To the right is the Chews Lane apartment block off Willis Street.

Right: The concrete canyon at the southern end of Lambton Quay shows the ANZ building on the left, the art deco building built for the Mutual Life and Citizens Assurance Company (1940) and a glimpse of the State Insurance Tower on Willis Street and the Westpac building (right) of 1974 vintage.

MANNERS STREET from Willis Street, the new expressway for city buses.

THE NATIONAL WAR MEMORIAL and Massey University (formerly the Dominion Museum and then the National Art Gallery Museum), with Mount Victoria on the horizon.

THE TERRACE from the Salamanca Road junction to Everton Terrace has a mix
of classic colonial residences balanced with later modern structures.

THE NORTHERN END OF THE TERRACE has slowly transformed over the decades from a street of grand Victorian residences to the hub of commerce. The Pohutukawa tree (centre) in front of the Wellington Club building was once behind a boundary hedge on Club property before The Terrace was widened.

THE HEART OF THE CAPITAL surrounded by tall buildings within the CBD. Willis Street and Customhouse Quay are on the right. The 18-storey Jellicoe Towers apartment block (left), built in 1965, was a pioneer of high-rise apartment blocks in Wellington. Below can be seen the tower of Antrim House (1905), a grand Edwardian house built for Robert Hannah the footwear retailer. The house has been the national headquarters of the New Zealand Historic Places Trust since 1981.

OVER PAGE: THE STAR BOATING CLUB building of 1885 (left) and the Wellington Rowing Club's building, 1894 (centre), on the edge of a man-made lagoon which was part of the harbour redevelopment. On the right is the new Wharewaka House which was opened on Waitangi Day, 2011. Behind is the steam-driven floating crane Hikitia which has been part of Wellington since arriving from Scotland in 1926.

THE CIVIC CENTRE. From left: the Michael Fowler Centre, the Town Hall, the Wellington City Council offices, the Wellington Public Library, the City Gallery, the Information Centre, Capital E and a café. In the foreground is the City to Sea pedestrian bridge over Jervois Quay.

Cuba Street has always been a colourful shopping strip. For 60 years electric trams fought for territory on the thoroughfare, first with horse-drawn traffic, then with motor vehicles. In 1969 the street between Dixon and Ghuznee Streets made history as the first shopping mall precinct in New Zealand. It is hard to imagine that the mall once accommodated parked cars on either side and a double set of tram tracks in the middle.

THE COURTENAY QUARTER towards the city with Mount Victoria homes on the right and the Basin Reserve on the left.

THE MUSEUM OF NEW ZEALAND Te Papa Tongarewa, which opened in February 1998, houses and displays the nation's treasures. Known as Te Papa, which means Our Place, it is an exploration of historical stories of New Zealand and its people.

Above: COURTENAY PLACE and Taranaki Street, the hub of theatre life in the city.

Left: CAMBRIDGE AND KENT TERRACES from the Basin Reserve, originally meant to be used as a canal to the Basin Reserve for ship repairs until the earthquake of 1855 raised the land.

Below: THE BASIN RESERVE is acknowledged as the best cricket oval in New Zealand thanks to the January 1855 earthquake which raised the land on the Huriwhenua Flat by several metres.

CHAFFERS MARINA by the old overseas passenger terminal is a deep-water, 185-berth facility opened in 1993. Chaffers Marina was named after the New Zealand Company's harbourmaster.

THE CLYDE QUAY marina and the Royal Port Nicholson Yacht Club (established 1883) on the seafront of Oriental Parade and (behind at right) the Kingsgate Hotel Wellington.

THE FREYBERG POOL was named after a famous son of Wellington, Sir Bernard Freyberg. This covered complex was opened in December 1963.

THE MOORED RAFT off Oriental Bay beach is a popular challenge for swimmers.

WHERE ORIENTAL PARADE MEETS ORIENTAL TERRACE is alive with sun seekers in the summer months.

MARATHON RUNNERS competing in the annual Round the Bays event pass along Oriental Parade early on a Sunday morning.

ORIENTAL BAY IS TODAY the Mediterranean of the south with people promenading from dawn to dusk, and cafés and restaurants with tables and chairs on the pavement. At night the water and the illuminated pine trees reflect the ever-growing wall of high-rise apartment blocks.

POINT JERNINGHAM AND ROSENEATH with Hataitai homes clinging to the hills behind.

Facing page: THE TOWN BELT on Mount Victoria, showing Hataitai Park on the right in the foreground.

HATAITAI where the hills are alive with homes.

GRETA POINT on the Evans Bay waterfront is now populated with modern apartment blocks.

BALAENA BAY (foreground) and little Karaka Bay, with a cascade of hills and houses above.

THE EVANS BAY MARINA and the Evans Bay Yacht and Motor Boat Club beyond. St Patrick's College, which moved to the site in 1979, is in the foreground and on the hill is Overton Terrace.

THE INDOOR COMMUNITY SPORTS CENTRE is a six-court centre at Cobham Park with a 10,000 m2 sports floor, on the verge of Evans Bay

THE WELLINGTON REGIONAL HOSPITAL'S new main building on Riddiford Street, Newtown. At top left is the junction of Riddiford Street with Rintoul Street, the centre of the Newtown shopping area.

THE SPLENDOUR OF GOVERNMENT HOUSE after restoration. Government House was built in 1910 to replace the old vice-regal residence in Parliament grounds which had been destroyed by fire. The first resident was Lord Islington (June 1910 to December 1912). It has a floor area of 4200 square metres.

LYALL BAY is a surf beach of wide acclaim.

Facing page (top): THE WELLINGTON INTERNATIONAL AIRPORT between Rongotai and the Miramar Peninsular.

Facing page (lower): THE INTERNATIONAL TERMINAL – 'The Rock' building was opened in November 2010. Copper panels cover the exterior, a radical departure from traditional airport design, which evoke the rocks and the marine life of the coast, also visible are the north pier (centre) and the main terminal building (right).

THE MIRAMAR PENINSULAR looking south, Maupuia Park (foreground) and Miramar Park (beyond) by where Wellywood is based in the centre of the photograph.

STRATHMORE PARK (foreground), towards Miramar with Miramar Park in the centre. On the right is Worser Bay, beyond are Karaka and Scorching Bays and the Maupuia headland.

SEATOUN PENINSULAR, Point Dorset, the former army station Fort Dorset, Seatoun and Seatoun Heights. Point Dorset is on the left with Barrett Reef in the distance.

TE WHANGANUI A TARA – The Great Harbour of Tara, is always busy with container ships, interisland ferries, launches and yachts entering *and leaving*. *Facing page:* The interislander ferry *Arahuru* heads into Wellington's natural deep water harbour, Port Nicholson.

POINT DORSET, Seatoun, with Breaker Bay on the left.

THE HOMES ON THE HILLS OF BROOKLYN – Magic views of the city.

FROM BERHAMPORE to Melrose to Rongotai, with the airport in the distance. The photograph shows Luxford Street (centre left), with Adelaide Road running across the centre from above Kingston.

LOOKING FROM ISLAND BAY down The Parade (centre), back to the city in the far distance. Derwent Street runs to the left.

THE ESPLANADE, ISLAND BAY, around past the Sirens Rocks to Owhiro Bay and to Sinclair Head.

Facing page: HAPPY VALLEY ROAD, with the Happy Valley Park and the Happy Valley School in the foreground at right.

ARO STREET (right foreground) to the the Kelburn campus of Victoria University on the fringe of the city, to Somes/Matiu Island in the distance and beyond to Petone and Lower Hutt City.

THE VICTORIA UNIVERSITY OF WELLINGTON, with the Hunter Building of late Gothic style, the first to be built on the campus in 1904, in the foreground of this view.

FROM KELBURN PARK to the cable car, to the homes on the slopes of the suburb of Northand.

AT THE TOP OF THE KELBURN CABLE CAR – The Upland Road terminus with the Wellington Cable Car Museum (right) and the Skyline restaurant on the left. Like San Francisco, the Wellington cable car climbs steeply upwards, from the city high-rise buildings below through tunnels and over viaducts to the residential suburb of Kelburn.

WEIR HOUSE, a Victoria University of Wellington hall of residence built in 1932 on Kelburn heights, stands above the Talavera station on the cable car line. Timber merchant William Weir bequeathed money for the building when he died in 1926. The Talavera station is where the two cable cars pass, the halfway point between the city and Kelburn.

Facing page: THE KARORI RESERVOIR AND DAM, completed in 1873, is now the home of Zealandia, the Karori Sanctuary Experience, Te Maraa Tane, which opened to the public in June 2001. It is the world's first fully fenced urban wildlife sanctuary and encloses regenerating forest. It is only 10 minutes from central Wellington. It is a unique pest-free sanctuary with over 35 kilometres of bush tracks and paths covering over 252 hectares of nature reserve. The placid waters of the reservoir are enhanced by the small neo-Gothic water-valve tower (1875), which once controlled the flow of water. The Kelburn Viaduct c1931 (left foreground) and Appleton Park (right foreground) can also be seen.

THE HEART OF THE SUBURB OF KARORI from Wrights Hill with Campbell Street running down the centre of this view. Ben Burn Park is the lovely green area.

THE KARORI SHOPPING MALL was the first shopping mall development in New Zealand, with off-street parking provided, in the early 1970s. The Post Shop can be seen on the corner of Karori Road and Beauchamp Street. The large red building to the right was formerly the Regent Theatre, now the headquarters of the Karori Bridge Club.

THE VITAL ARTERY OF NEW ZEALAND'S LARGEST SUBURB – Looking back down Karori Road from Makara Road. Karori Park is on the left.

WADESTOWN – Barnard Street is at the foot of this view, then Anne and Sefton Streets and beyond to Oban Crescent. Above the railway line cutting is Bowen Hospital.

THE HILLS OF WADESTOWN – St Luke's Anglican Church on Wadestown Road can be seen on the left.
The view is towards the Town Belt and the port. The cruise liner *Deutschland* is berthed at Aotea Quay.

Right: THE KHANDALLAH TENNIS AND SQUASH CLUB on Delhi Crescent. Behind is Station Road (centre) with the railway line, Box Hill and Burma Road beyond.

Below: THIS VIEW OF KHANDALLAH shows Madras Street in the foreground, Gurkha Crescent (centre) with Shastri Terrace on the right. On the hills to the right are the homes of Rangoon Heights and Broadmeadows.

A BIRD'S–EYE VIEW OF KHANDALLAH shows Rama Crescent (left), Nairnville Park in the centre distance and Nicholson Road (right foreground). In the distance (left) is Crofton Downs and spreading into the distant hills are the homes of Ngaio.

THE HEART OF NGAIO: The junction of Ottawa and Khandallah Roads with Conway Street is in the foreground, with Tarikaka Street to the left and the Nairnville Park and Recreation Centre top left. The Ngaio School is on the right.

LOOKING SOUTH over Paparangi, Newlands and Johnsonville to the city in the distance. State Highway One heads into Wellington with the turn-off to the shopping centre of Johnsonville on the right.

LOVELY LOWRY BAY with Sorrento Bay in the foreground and the Francis Bell Reserve behind.

LOOKING FROM DAYS BAY to Rona Bay, Eastbourne, Webb Point, Robinsons Bay and Muritai. Wellesley College is in the foreground. This is the road that leads to the Pencarrow lighthouse at Wellington Heads. Pencarrow was the first coastal light to be operated in New Zealand on 1 January 1850. The light shone from a small keeper's cottage until a cast-iron kitset lighthouse arrived from Britain in 1858. It was the first permanent lighthouse in the country.

DAYS BAY – Williams Park and the Days Bay wharf where the East by West catamaran *DominionPost* ferries have been taking commuters to the city since 1989.

ROBINSON BAY, EASTBOURNE – homes by the sea.

EASTBOURNE, the Rona Bay wharf, the Village Corner Shopping Centre and the public pool on Marine Parade.

IN A SECLUDED VALLEY IS WAINUIOMATA, over the hill from Lower Hutt City. The Main Road runs across the photograph from far right to left

THE PETONE EARLY SETTLERS' MUSEUM on the Esplanade by Buick Street was built in 1940 as the Wellington Provincial Centennial Memorial. It commemorates the landing at Petone Beach of settlers from the immigrant ships *Cuba* and *Aurora* in January 1840.

OVERLOOKING PETONE with North Park (left foreground) the Petone Rugby Football Club's grounds, and the Petone Recreation Ground (right foreground), the Shandon Golf Course (top left) and, in the distance, Seaview and Point Howard. The Petone Working Men's Club (foreground) on Udy Street and the McKenzie Swimming Pool beyond also on Udy Street.

PETONE BY THE SEA – (from the foreshore on the left:) The Esplanade, Adelaide and Jackson Streets running up the photograph and Collins Street running across in the foreground. The Petone Recreation Ground is at top right.

THE EWEN BRIDGE, gateway to Lower Hutt from the south. This bridge, opened in 1995, is the seventh to span the river at the entrance to Lower Hutt City.

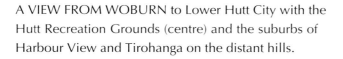

A VIEW FROM WOBURN to Lower Hutt City with the Hutt Recreation Grounds (centre) and the suburbs of Harbour View and Tirohanga on the distant hills.

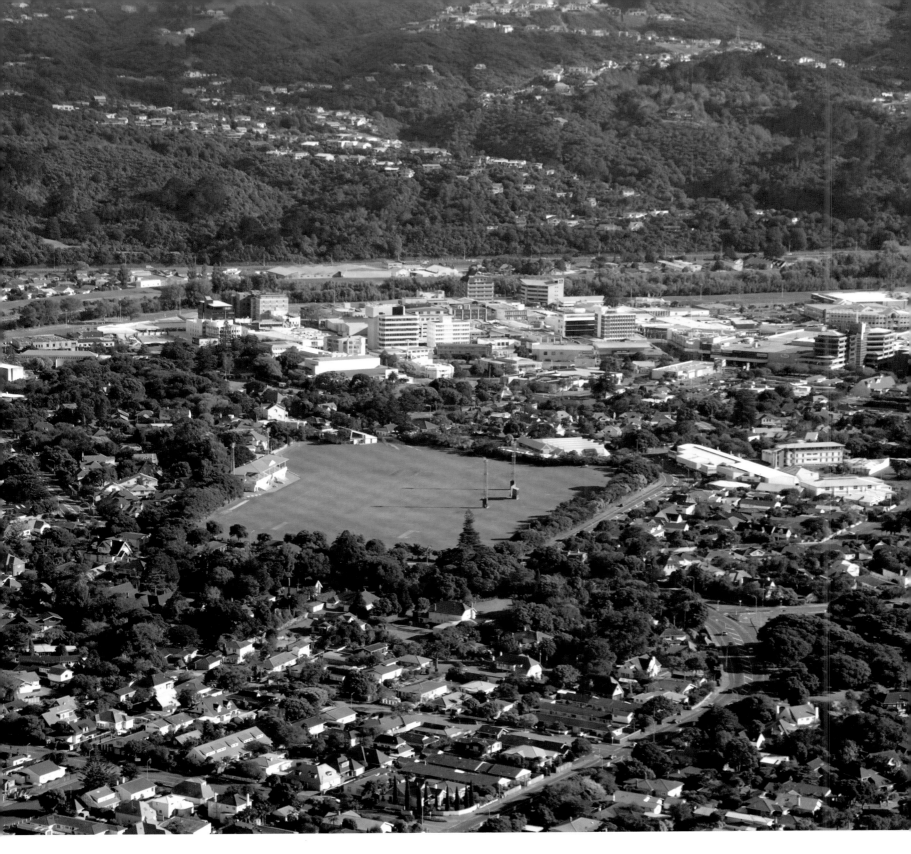

THE CENTRAL CITY BUSINESS DISTRICT of Lower Hutt City with the Hutt River in the foreground.

THE WESTERN HUTT ROAD heads north past the streets of Taita on the other side of the Hutt River.

LOOKING UP STOKES VALLEY; the Eastern Hutt Road runs across in the foreground.

ST PATRICK'S COLLEGE at Silverstream

THE ROYAL WELLINGTON GOLF CLUB (established 1895) has been part of Heretaunga since 1905.

THE ENTRANCE TO THE CITY OF UPPER HUTT from River Road into Gibbons Street. In the foreground is Riverbank Park and on the left (centre) is Oxford Park and the Oxford Crescent School.

THE CENTRAL BUSINESS DISTRICT OF PORIRUA with the Porirua Stream and the railway station in the foreground. Titahi Bay Road curves round the North City Shopping Centre (top left), first opened in 1991 as the K-Mart Plaza. Post-Second-World-War housing developments saw rapid growth from a village, with Porirua becoming a city in 1965.

THE CENTRE OF PORIRUA CITY with the harbour basin to the north. Titahi Bay Road is on the left, Lytttelton Avenue runs across the city centre in the foreground. Porirua School is at left centre. On the right is State Highway One and the North Island main trunk railway line.

LOOKING SOUTH FROM THE ENTRANCE TO PORIRUA HARBOUR over the Onepoto Peninsula, Whitireia Park, Titahi Bay, to Onepoto and Kura Parks, the Porirua Scenic Reserve (in the distance, left) and Stuart Park (on the coast on the right beyond Titahi Bay) to Mana Island on the horizon.

THE PLACID WATERS OF THE PAUATAHANUI ARM of Porirua Harbour from Bradeys and Browns Bays with Whitby (foreground) to Camborne, Plimmerton and Te Rewarewa Point in the far distance at right.

THE MANA MARINA at Deep Water Point, home of the Mana Cruising Club. The railway and motorway bridges cross the entrance to the Pauatahanui arm of the Porirua Harbour and the suburb of Camborne reaches to the hills.

PLIMMERTON AND KAREHANA BAY with the Plimmerton Boating Club (foreground at right), Karehana and the Karehana Bay Scenic Reserve (left foreground), looking back along Moana Road and Sunset Parade to Camborne and Mana in the distance.

THE CENTENNIAL ocean highway hugs the coastline between Pukerua Bay (facing page, far left) and Paekakariki while the North Island main trunk railway snakes its way through many tunnels above the highway. A Ganz Mavag electric unit heads for Waikanae.

PAEKAKARIKI IS AN OLD RAILWAY TOWNSHIP remembered in songs and is where the old New Zealand Railways 'Paekok Pie' was once famous when steam trains stopped for refreshments.

THE PAEKAKARIKI SURF CLUB and holiday park by the Wainui Stream at the southern end of Queen Elizabeth Park on the Kapiti Coast.

QUEEN ELIZABETH PARK by the mouth of the Whareroa Stream. This beach area at the end of Whareroa Road is also the terminus of the Wellington Tramway Museum's 1.85-kilometres-long electric tramway which runs from within the Memorial Gates at the entrance to Queen Elizabeth Park near MacKays Crossing to this picnic area on the coast.

Facing page: RAUMATI BEACH IS A SPLENDID SEASIDE HAVEN with lovely homes and gardens.

Above: By the mouth of the Wharemauki Stream, with the Marine Gardens and the shopping centre behind. The first waterfront sub-divisions on the Kapiti Coast were at Raumati in 1906.

Left: PARAPARAUMU BEACH with MacLean Park (foreground), the Paraparaumu golf course (left) and the Paraparaumu Airport on the right and beyond, the Coastlands Shopping Centre.

Below: The Kapiti Island ferry returning to Paraparaumu Beach. The island is pest and predator free, and the Department of Conservation issues permits for people to visit the island's nature reserve. Only 50 people are allowed on Kapiti Island, only 5 kilometres off the coast, each day.

WAIKANAE BEACH is a lovely stretch of golden sand on the Kapiti Coast, populated by permanent residents and Wellingtonians seeking a more temperate climate for relaxation.

Above: Oratia Street is on the left and Waiheke Street on the right with Tutere Street running north to south and the Waimanu Wildlife Refuge Lagoon beyond.

Houses on Tutere Street with beachfront properties, Eruni Street is (centre), running toward the widlife refuge Waimeha Lagoon beyond.

Right: The Waikanae Boating Club on Tutere Street is a mecca for Waikanae boaties. Te Moana Road can be seen in the distance at top left.

You can't beat Wellington on a good day!